DON'T SLURP YOUR SOUP!

What to do
when your mom or dad says. . .
"DON'T SLURP YOUR SOUP!"

By
JOY WILT BERRY

Living Skills Press
Fallbrook, California

Distributed by:

Word, Incorporated
4800 W. Waco Drive
Waco, TX 76703

Dear Parents:

"DON'T SLURP YOUR SOUP!" Have you ever said this to your children and had them ask you, "Why?"

You could answer this question by saying, "Because I told you so!" But there really is a better answer.

This issue is a matter of etiquette. Etiquette is not just an optional part of everyday living. In situations involving relationships, etiquette is essential. It is the guideline that shows us how to act in pleasing and acceptable ways, and it tells us how to be gracious around other people. Sound etiquette is based on three very important principles:

Do unto others as you would have them do unto you. Every one of us has a deep need to be treated with kindness and respect. If we hope to receive kindness and respect from other people, we must treat them with the same. Centered in this truth is the balance between "what's good for me" and "what's good for you," a balance that is necessary for the survival and growth of any human relationship.

Beauty is as beauty does. This means that our personal beauty depends on our behavior rather than on our physical appearance. In other words, it is how we act rather than how we appear that makes us ugly or beautiful. No matter what we look like, crude behavior can make us ugly, while gracious behavior can make us beautiful in a very special way.

A thing of beauty is a joy forever! Think about it. When you are around something that is ugly, you probably feel sad and depressed. On the other hand, when you are around something that is beautiful, you probably feel inspired and happy.

It is the same way with people. Being around a person who is ugly because of crude behavior is often sad and depressing.

3

However, being around a person who is beautiful because of gracious behavior is often inspiring and uplifting. Generally speaking, people do not want to be around a person who makes them feel depressed. Instead, they want to be around someone who makes them feel good.

If we are gracious, others will desire rather than resist our companionship. This is important as all of us are social beings.

Your children come into the world as social beings possessing specific social needs. Accompanying these needs are your children's innate abilities to get their needs met, but these abilities are undeveloped. One of your jobs as parents is to facilitate the development of these abilities. You can accomplish this by doing these things:

1. Help your children observe and evaluate their own behavior as it relates to others.
2. Bring your children into a basic understanding of the three principles mentioned above.
3. Help your children clarify social expectations.
4. Expose your children to guidelines that can enable them to meet valid social expectations.

This book can help you achieve these things. If you will use it systematically (as part of a continuing program) or as a resource (to be used whenever the need for it arises), you and your children will experience some very positive results.

With your help, your children can and will know exactly what you mean when you say **"DON'T SLURP YOUR SOUP!"** and will be able to respond graciously.

Sincerely,

Joy Wilt Berry

Has your mother or father ever told you. . .

Whenever this happens, do you wonder. . .

If any of this sounds familiar to you, you are going to **love** this book!

Because it will tell you about slurping your soup and other things you should avoid doing when eating with other people.

BEGINNING A MEAL WITH OTHER PEOPLE

This is Peter Pig. Peter refuses to clean himself up before he sits down to eat a meal.

Peter does not care about the people who will be eating with him. Without asking anyone, he sits where he wants to and begins eating before anyone has had a chance to get situated. Peter is not very gracious.

Whenever you begin a meal, you can be gracious by doing these things:

Make sure that you are neat and clean before coming to the table. Wash your face and hands, and change your clothes if they are badly soiled.

Wait for the host or hostess to tell you where to sit before you sit down. (A host is a man who invites people to come to his home as his guests. A hostess is a woman who invites people to come to her home as her guests.) If you are in a situation where there is no host or hostess, let the person who is in charge of the meal tell you where to sit.

Once you are seated at the table, wait to see if someone is going to say grace. If someone does, be reverent and respectful during the prayer.

Pick up your napkin and put it in your lap.
Keep it there during the meal and use it to wipe
your hands or mouth whenever necessary.

Make sure that every person at the table has received a fair share of food before you begin to eat.

Let the host, hostess, or person in charge of the meal tell you when to begin eating. If nothing is said, begin eating when he or she begins.

EATING WITH OTHER PEOPLE

Peter Pig is rude and crude when he eats with other people. His only concern is himself and his needs.

Peter is never concerned about the people with whom he is eating. He does not care whether or not he offends them. Peter is not very gracious.

Whenever you eat with other people, you can be gracious by doing these things:

Ask the people around you kindly to pass things that are out of your reach; then, thank them when they respond to your request.

Whenever you are asked, pass things as quickly
and as kindly as possible.

If you need to pass an object with a handle, such as a cup or utensil, pass it with the handle pointing toward the other person.

If you need to pass something that is very hot or cold, set it down next to the person so that it may be picked up by its handles or with some pot-holders. If something is too hot or heavy to pass, offer to put some of the food onto the plate for the person.

Try not to burp or hiccup while you are eating. If you should accidentally do either one, politely say, "Excuse me."

If you must sneeze or cough while you are at the
table, turn your head away from the food and
cover your mouth.

Try not to crowd the people around you by taking more than your share of table space or by putting your elbows on the table.

Try not to make a mess around you when you eat.

Try not to stuff your mouth full of food. Also, avoid talking when you have something in your mouth.

Try to eat quietly. Avoid slurping things or chewing with your mouth open.

USING YOUR DINNERWARE PROPERLY

Peter Pig does not know how to use the plates,
bowls, and glasses that are set in front of him, and
so he abuses them.

Peter Pig does not know how to use silverware and so he abuses it as well. Peter is not very gracious.

Plates, bowls, glasses, and utensils can make your eating easier and more fun if you learn how to use them in the right way.

In regard to **plates** and **bowls,** learn how each one is to be used and then use it properly.

1. Salad plate, for salads
2. Soup bowl, for soup
3. Dinner plate, for the main meal
4. Bread plate, for bread and butter
5. Dessert bowl, for desserts
6. Dessert plate, for dessert or to set dessert bowl on

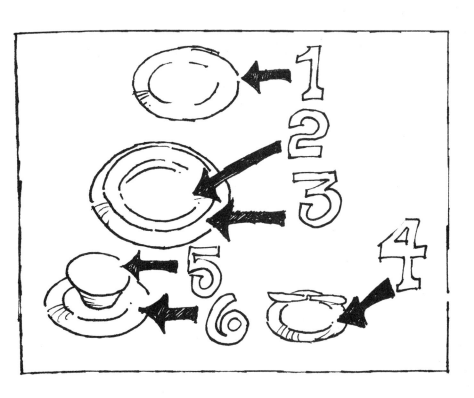

Learn how to use each **glass** and **cup** and then use each one properly.

1. Water glass, usually the largest
2. Beverage glass, for milk or juice
3. Coffee cup or teacup and saucer, for coffee or tea.

BLiPPP

Learn how each piece of **silverware** is to be
used and then use it properly.

1. Soup spoon, for soup or broth
2. Salad or fish fork, for salad or fish (if one of them is served before the main meal)
3. Salad or fish knife
4. Dinner fork, for the main meal
5. Dinner knife, usually for meat
6. Butter knife
7. Dessert spoon, for dessert
8. Dessert fork, for dessert

Use your silverware in the proper order. Begin with the pieces farthest from your plate and work in. If you are not sure what utensil to start with, watch to see what your host or hostess does.

Handle your food with your silverware, unless the food is "finger food" (food that is meant to be picked up with your fingers).

If you are served something that needs to be cut into smaller pieces, do these things:

Step 1

Use your fork to hold your food in place. Note that you do not make a fist around an upright fork, but rather hold the fork gently at an angle, as shown in the illustration.

Step 2

Use your knife to cut the food.

Step 3

After you have cut off one piece of food, lay your knife down on the edge of your plate, with the cutting edge to the inside. Cut only one piece of food at a time.

Step 4

Put the piece of food into your mouth with your fork. Put only one piece of food into your mouth at a time.

If you must take something out of your mouth, like gristle, a bone, or a seed:

Carefully place it on your spoon.

After you have put the gristle, bone, or seed onto
your spoon:

Empty it onto your plate.

While you are eating, put the utensils you are using on the edge of your plate. Try not to lay them down on the table at anytime.

When you have finished eating, put your utensils over the center of your plate, handles to the right. The fork, tines up, is placed nearest you; the knife blade faces the fork. Whenever bowls are used, put the utensils in the bowl when you have finished eating.

AFTER THE MEAL

When you are ready to leave the table, ask to be excused.

Before you leave the table, remember to thank the person who was kind enough to prepare your food.

THE END of not knowing proper table manners.